TEA TIME WITH GOD

Treasures of the Heart

Debi Ayers

WESTBOW
PRESS®
A DIVISION OF THOMAS NELSON
& ZONDERVAN

Scripture quotations marked NKJV are taken from the New King James Version®. Copyright © 1982 by Thomas Nelson. Used by permission. All rights reserved.

Scripture quotations marked TLB are taken from The Living Bible Copyright © 1971 by Tyndale House Foundation. Used by permission of Tyndale House Publishers Inc., Carol Stream, Illinois 60188. All rights reserved. The Living Bible, TLB, and the The Living Bible logo are registered trademarks of Tyndale House Publishers.

This book is a work of non-fiction. Unless otherwise noted, the author and the publisher make no explicit guarantees as to the accuracy of the information contained in this book and in some cases, names of people and places have been altered to protect their privacy.

WestBow Press books may be ordered through booksellers or by contacting:

WestBow Press
A Division of Thomas Nelson & Zondervan
1663 Liberty Drive
Bloomington, IN 47403
www.westbowpress.com
1 (866) 928-1240

Because of the dynamic nature of the Internet, any web addresses or links contained in this book may have changed since publication and may no longer be valid. The views expressed in this work are solely those of the author and do not necessarily reflect the views of the publisher, and the publisher hereby disclaims any responsibility for them.

Any people depicted in stock imagery provided by Getty Images are models, and such images are being used for illustrative purposes only. Certain stock imagery © Getty Images.

ISBN: 978-1-9736-4867-3 (sc)
ISBN: 978-1-9736-4869-7 (hc)
ISBN: 978-1-9736-4868-0 (e)

Library of Congress Control Number: 2018914740

Print information available on the last page.

WestBow Press rev. date: 01/07/2019

Contents

Foreword

TEA TIME WITH GOD IS A LONG-ANTICIPATED BOOK THAT IS the antidote of living in a helter-skelter world—one that feels as if we are on a perpetual merry-go-round that never seems to stop, let alone slow down. Our society today is moving at an ever-increasing pace. Everyone is in such a hurry and striving to multitask and accomplish more and more. In the end, we are losing peace and joy in our lives.

Thankfully, Debi Ayers has learned balance to all of this madness by applying God's Word to her life. She has discovered peace—which is what society is sorely missing—by trusting God in the midst of life's storms. God has proven to be faithful to her when she applied Psalm 46:10, "Be still, and know that I am God." Debi skillfully relates in this book her own story, which includes overwhelming challenges, tests, and trials. She then shares how her life has been transformed by discovering life-changing intimacy with God.

Dear friends, there are within this book "golden nuggets" that include truth and blessings for all who choose to apply them to their own lives. Whether you are facing a season of dryness, despair, or hopelessness in your own life or just want to go deeper in your personal relationship with our heavenly

Father, then I encourage you to take the time and read this book. Remember, you were born for such a time as this. Enjoy the journey!

Robert (Bob) J. Farrar

Dedication

FIRSTLY, I WANT TO THANK MY GOD! MY HEART IS FILLED with gratefulness to Him for His leading, guidance, and direction of this book. My prayer is that every reader receives a new and fresh revelation of who Jesus Christ is in his or her own life.

Secondly, although this book is written for others to find their own peace with God in trials and tribulations, it is especially written for my precious children, for you to gain insight from the stories on the pages of this book. My greatest joy in life has been being your mother, and there are no words to express my true love for you nor how proud I am of who you have become!

As a grandmother, I have been given a new and fresh joy that keeps my heart full. For our precious granddaughter and all future grandchildren, I pray that this book encourages you to pursue the plans God has for your lives. Keep Him first in all you do, and you will accomplish much. Always know and remember how much Jesus loves you!

For my siblings, this book is intended to be a tribute to our loving parents. I pray you will glean more peace and comfort as you read of the special moments God gave us through their last days here on earth. May it bring peace, comfort, joy, and thankfulness to your hearts as you remember the two people who gave us life, loved us, and cared for us in such special ways!

For my niece and nephews, I do not need to tell you how much you were loved by your grandparents, for they showed you that love in many ways. Only you know the true essence of that love for your individual hearts. Always remember the diverse ways they showed you how special you were to them.

Introduction

THIS BOOK EXPRESSES THE WAY IN WHICH GOD IS ALWAYS blessing us, especially in our time of need. God is daily in our midst, leading us, guiding our steps, consoling our hearts, and protecting us. It doesn't matter how dire our situation appears in the natural; in the supernatural God is always in the center of it.

My hope in sharing these personal stories is to help each reader identify and know that God, not being a respecter of persons, is always helping each one of us in our time of need. Be encouraged to look for God in the center of your circumstance, and know that He may be in the smallest detail of your day, such as a smile, a hug, or an encouraging word.

CHAPTER 1

Tea Time with God

TEA TIME—AH YES, TEA TIME. IT ALWAYS CREATES AN atmosphere of refuge for me. Whether I am with family, friends, or sharing "a spot of tea" with strangers at an event, I always feel that I need to just sit still, relax, and breathe. Hence, the title of this book, *Tea Time with God*. To be able to sit and remember the scripture "Stand still [be still] and know that I am God" (Psalm 46:10)[1] enables me to clear my mind of many emotions and understand that God is in control of every aspect of my life. And isn't that the beginning of much wisdom? In the presence of God is where all things change, including our hearts. Recently, while praying for someone, I heard in my spirit "God's presence will awaken the Spirit within you." Wow! Isn't that the truth! And isn't it a truth that we need to remember when we are enduring trial or tribulation?

One of my favorite memories is attending a tea with my mother, which was held at one of our favorite resorts. The fresh aroma of flavored teas and the delicate sandwiches and desserts were comforting, but the live piano music is what added to our enjoyment. My mom was always at a piano, whether it was teaching a student or playing for church services, weddings, funerals, etc. Thus it was a tremendous treat for her to sit and listen to someone else expressing their talent. Watching her relax to the point of visible peacefulness is still a precious memory to me.

Do you realize we experience this same peacefulness when we share a cup of tea with God Himself? Just sitting in the stillness of His presence, or reading His Word, or praying silently over the aroma and warmth of the tea fills me with His joy and His peace.

Don't allow the title to dissuade you from reading any further, for the significance of this title is different for each person. It requires taking a moment to stop what you are doing and notice what God is doing in that moment.

Tea time for my husband is going to the mountains and sitting quietly in the beauty of God's creation. He will not be found sipping a cup of tea, but he may be seen holding a cup of coffee. His joy is found there, where he can clearly hear the voice of God while he sits in His presence, uninterrupted.

God's presence may be found in anything, such as the stillness of the night, the sound of water trickling in a brook, the butterfly gently gliding in the air, the beauty of the snowcapped mountains, the reflection of majestic mountains in a crystal-clear lake, a shared hug with a loved one, the gentle kiss to a newborn's precious face, or the hug of an enthusiastic toddler with his voice bellowing, "I love you!" You see, all these things bring love, peace, and joy from God our Father to us, His children. We just need to take a moment to recognize His hand at work.

Many songs have been written that define the results of being in the company of God. His presence heals a broken heart, banishes worry and concern, removes oppression and depression, gives hope to the hopeless, and removes the burdens that weigh us down. Why wouldn't we want to stay in His presence? Isaiah 9:6[2] calls Jesus the Prince of Peace.

My prayer is that each reader will experience their own *Tea Time with God* as he or she journeys through the pages of this book.

CHAPTER 2

A Woman of God

Proverbs 31[1]

[1] THESE ARE THE WISE SAYINGS OF KING LEMUEL OF MASSA, taught to him at his mother's knee: [2] O my son, whom I have dedicated to the Lord, [3] do not spend your time with women—the royal pathway to destruction. [4] And it is not for kings, O Lemuel, to drink wine and whiskey. [5] For if they drink, they may forget their duties and be unable to give justice to those who are oppressed. [6-7] Hard liquor is for sick men at the brink of death, and wine for those in deep depression. Let them drink to forget their poverty and misery.

[8] You should defend those who cannot help themselves. [9] Yes, speak up for the poor and helpless, and see that they get justice. [10] If you can find a truly good wife, she is worth more than precious gems! [11] Her husband can trust her, and she will

richly satisfy his needs. ¹² She will not hinder him but help him all her life. ¹³ She finds wool and flax and busily spins it. ¹⁴ She buys imported foods brought by ship from distant ports. ¹⁵ She gets up before dawn to prepare breakfast for her household and plans the day's work for her servant girls. ¹⁶ She goes out to inspect a field and buys it; with her own hands she plants a vineyard. ¹⁷ She is energetic, a hard worker, ¹⁸ and watches for bargains. She works far into the night!

¹⁹⁻²⁰ She sews for the poor and generously helps those in need. ²¹ She has no fear of winter for her household, for she has made warm clothes for all of them. ²² She also upholsters with finest tapestry; her own clothing is beautifully made—a purple gown of pure linen. ²³ Her husband is well known, for he sits in the council chamber with the other civic leaders. ²⁴ She makes belted linen garments to sell to the merchants. ²⁵ She is a woman of strength and dignity and has no fear of old age. ²⁶ When she speaks, her words are wise, and kindness is the rule for everything she says. ²⁷ She watches carefully all that goes on throughout her household and is never lazy. ²⁸ Her children stand and bless her; so does her husband. He praises her with these words: ²⁹ "There are many fine women in the world, but you are the best of them all!" ³⁰ Charm can be deceptive and beauty doesn't last, but a woman who fears and reverences God shall be greatly praised. ³¹ Praise her for the many fine things she does. These good deeds of hers shall bring her honor and recognition from people of importance.

CHAPTER 3

A Mother's Love

IT IS ONLY FITTING FOR ME TO BEGIN THIS BOOK WITH A special kind of love, a mother's love. This love cannot be explained; it is only experienced. All mothers know this is a love that God bestows upon our hearts and realize that such an unconditional love can only come from God Himself. I was blessed to have an example of this kind of love in my life—my own dear mother, a true woman of God!

Why is it that we don't know everything about people or appreciate them enough until they are gone? My only answer to date is that there are secrets and treasures in intimate love that we only share with close family and friends. Too many times we take one another for granted and do not take advantage of the time we are given. Our joy in knowing our loved ones comes from spending time with them, so never waste a moment that God gives you!

Sometimes I feel as if time has stood still since we received the news that my mother was losing her second battle with cancer and had just months to live. But it was during that time that God's love and mercy was shed among many of us. By His grace, numerous friends and family members had special time with Mom before she passed on from this life into glory. It is my desire to share some of the special moments I experienced with my beloved mother while she was transitioning to the life hereafter. In sharing these memories, my prayer and hope for you is that you will *not* take for granted each moment you have with your own loved ones today. Be encouraged that God does pour out His love upon you when you need it the most, no matter what the circumstance. Again, be open to the God encounters in your life, and you will never regret. What will remain with you will be "treasures of the heart."

CHAPTER 4

A Mother's Journey

My mother was getting so excited, knowing she only had several months left before hitting the ever-so-desired five-year mark of being free from breast cancer. She was looking forward to saying "I am cancer free" and having no more worries. Yet, on a scheduled visit for a liver biopsy, she was hospitalized due to feeling extremely ill and having a high fever. Watching her go through more tests and not knowing what the diagnosis would be caused us to start fretting. At that point, Mom confided in me that God had previously promised her she would not die of breast cancer. With our eyes, hearts, and hands locked into place, we agreed that this would not be a death sentence.

It was just like God to have Mom and Dad's pastor and his wife visiting her when the news arrived of the test results. These two people were not just pastors to my parents, they were extraordinary friends. They were the kind of friends with whom my parents, without needing words, could discern each other's thoughts and needs—a gift given by the Holy Spirit. As I walked into the room, one of Mom's doctors followed me. I could see the troubled look on the doctor's face, so I stood erect, ready to face the giant at hand as we heard the words *metastasis bone cancer*. Mom and I tried to stand strong for one another when we heard this, but nothing ever prepares you for the C-word, does it—especially the second time around, when you know the statistics. What a gift God gave us at that moment. The pastor said, "Let us have a word of prayer." We all joined hands, including that doctor, while our pastor friend requested God's hand of mercy and grace. Because of that prayer, a boldness rose within me as I looked into Mom's eyes, and I reassured her, "We will get through this." As I look back now, I recall that neither of us cried; we were being strong for each other. I guess I can truly say "Like mother, like daughter" in this respect. I knew we both believed that God was in control, and we were going to trust Him to bring us through, no matter what!

After more testing during Mom's hospital stay, the diagnosis became grimmer. We were told that Mom also had lung fibrosis and liver disease, which prompted additional doctors to become involved. At this point I could share the doubt and unbelief we all experienced, and the pain that Mom endured, but I would rather share what God did in our midst during this trial, for His mercy endures forever (Jeremiah 33:11).[2]

One day I was sitting at Mom's bedside and we were quietly talking, when like a flash, a nurse came into the room.

She shut the door with her back and leaned against the door. The nurse took a deep breath and then spoke: "I just needed some peace." It washed all over me at that moment and still brings tears to my eyes as I write this, *God's peace was entirely enveloping that room*! What a blessing to know that a stranger found solace in my mother's hospital room. When that nurse needed a refuge, she knew where she could hide.

Philippians 4:6–7 exploded in that hospital room that week. It says, "Don't worry about anything; instead, pray about everything; tell God your needs and don't forget to thank Him for His answers. If you do this you will experience God's peace, which is far more wonderful than the human mind can understand. His peace will keep your thoughts and your hearts quiet and at rest as you trust in Christ Jesus."[1]

Looking back to verses 4 and 5, in the same translation, reminds me of another story. Philippians 4:4–5 says, "Always be full of joy in the Lord; I say it again, rejoice! Let everyone see that you are unselfish and considerate in all you do. Remember that the Lord is coming soon."[1]

With all the questionable thoughts and fears within our family, we were still trusting God and His perfect plan. Doing this enabled us to treat all who entered Mom's room with respect, not just for their positions, but for each of them as a person. We were doing the "let everyone see that you are unselfish and considerate in all you do." In the midst of a battle, we still need to treat others correctly. It wasn't surprising to me that when Mom was being discharged from the hospital several nurses commented to us that they wished all their patients and families were like ours. All that was left to do was to smile, share hugs, and thank God for His peace and favor within us.

Mom was always walking in love towards others. She was the visible example of Ephesians 5:1[2]—Walk in Love—"Therefore be imitators of God as dear children."

Mom always treated people the same, including her children. There was no favoritism shown between my siblings and me; Mom was always fair. For this reason alone I know that my siblings have similar stories, but I am relating only mine here, firsthand. Mom always knew when something was wrong in my life, usually when I was at my breaking point. She would always find me so that we were alone, and with those loving, caring eyes would ask me the question, "What is wrong?" Just the love pouring from her eyes would cause me to stop and take a breath, forcing me to think about my life at that moment, and sure enough, the tears would flow. Mom always had the best encouragement and wisdom, so that when she left she took all my burdens with her. You know that is our God; Mom was an example of His hands extended every time. Now, back to her story.

For the next six months, Mom went for chemotherapy treatments on a regular basis, along with all the testing that goes along with it. At the end of the six months, the doctor informed her and the family that she was "a very sick lady." He advised us to go home and call hospice. Wow—some doctors have the best bedside manner! Yet the question remained: What do you do with those words? This doctor had just pronounced a death sentence to my mother! I know what God's Word tells us, that death and life are in the power of the tongue (Proverbs 18:21).[2]

There were, and always will be, the friends who would ask, "Whose report are you going to believe, the doctor's or the Great Physician's?" Of course I wanted to believe that God was still going to heal my mother, and I just knew He would use this miracle as a salvation tool in our family! But in reality, God did not heal my mother until He took her to Heaven. However, my mother's journey from this earth to her Heavenly home was a beautiful experience and one that needs to be told. But first, let us think about who she was to us.

One of the many great attributes that Mom had was to be a good listener. God filled her mouth with godly wisdom and advice for many that crossed her path. We have heard not only from family members telling us how Mom blessed them over the years, but many others shared their testimonies of how Mom helped them through personal crisis. Additionally, those who are now adults, shared their moments of teenage crisis when Mom was their piano teacher. We saw it all as a gift from God. Months after her passing from this life to Heaven, Mom's dental hygienist cried with me as she began sharing how many times Mom had listened and given her advice while at her dental appointments. Mom was open for God to use her in any way and at any time He so desired.

Days after the funeral our family was going through Mom's things, and we found a blank journal with her friend's name on it. We sent it to her and soon received a note back saying that Mom always knew when she needed another one. This friend had written in a journal all her life, and Mom had been instrumental in providing her with books just at the time a new one was needed. My thought at this moment was that Mom was still blessing others, only now from Heaven.

When we found Mom's card box, there were cards she had purchased for certain individuals but not sent. We mailed them for her, only to receive praise for Mom from all of them. As only God can, He was healing my heart when we did this! Thank you, God, for bringing so much joy to others through my beloved mother!

CHAPTER 5

The Last Thanksgiving

Mom's favorite holiday was Thanksgiving. This story is to show you how brave and courageous my mother really was. She was told in October that she had bone cancer, along with the other diseases previously mentioned. But in November she insisted on preparing the holiday meal for our family. That year was different, with everyone feeling so apprehensive about the future. As Mom began the blessing over the meal, it filled our hearts with an intense love for her as we listened to her eloquent prayer. We could literally feel her heart of love for all of us! There were usually a few tears shed during the blessing at special occasions when the family got together, but they were always tears of joy and thankfulness. The blessing said over the food always included thankfulness for each member at the table. But that year it was as if Mom was letting us know she realized it would be her last Thanksgiving with her beloved family. Her words of endearment penetrated our hearts and prompted the presence of the Lord in such a precious form that there were no dry eyes at that table.

Today I say with sadness that it was the last Thanksgiving we shared with our sweet mother. But the faith my mother instilled in me and showed me with her life arrests my soul with anticipation for "the marriage supper of the Lamb," where I will sit again with my own dear mother! You see, my extra blessing is knowing that Mom is not just in my past but in my future too! The same is for anyone who has lost a loved one—as long as that circle is unbroken, we will see that person again!

What do I mean about the unbroken circle? If you and your loved ones have received Jesus as your Savior, then it is true that you will one day be together again for the rest of eternity. If you knew my mother, then you knew it was her wish not to let the circle be broken. She desired that we would all join her in Heaven for eternity, friends and family alike. We will meet her there!

In God's mercy and grace, He gave me these scriptures when Mom passed on:

Isaiah 57:1-2:[1] "[1]The good men perish; the godly die before their time, and no one seems to care or wonder why. No one seems to realize that God is taking them away from evil days ahead. [2]For the godly who die shall rest in peace."

Thank you Father, that Mom is resting in complete peace and joy!

"Oh Death, where is thy sting" (1 Corinthians 15:55.)[2] This verse crossed my mind many times before her death, along with "To be absent from the body is to be present with the Lord" (2 Corinthians 5:8).[2]

Although these scriptures help heal my heart, I miss my mother and now my father too! But these scriptures bring joy to my heart, because I know my parents are free of all pain and living in more joy than any of us has experienced yet. And the expectation of seeing them again may elude the unbeliever, but as a person who has received Jesus Christ as my personal Savior, I *know* that I will see them again and believe it won't be long now!

CHAPTER 6

Friendship in Grief

You may know the scripture of Proverbs 18:24:[2] "But there is a friend who sticks closer than a brother." We know that friend is Jesus, but here is a story that shows how God sends His love through people.

A few weeks after Mom's passing, a very dear friend handed me a gold box and just smiled. When I opened it, I saw a red rope bracelet with these words engraved on it: Love You More. Through choking tears, I began telling her that since Mom had been battling sickness she had never let any of our family go out the door without saying those words to us. And her favorite color had been red. Astonished, my friend just held me and cried with me. All she knew before this moment was that God had told her to get it for me. Still today, when I see that bracelet, I can see Mom standing by Jesus, compelling Him to send this one last message: I Love You More!

My response? I love you too, Mom!

CHAPTER 7

Prayers for Healing

EVERYONE WAS PRAYING FOR MY MOTHER'S HEALING. FRIENDS and family were contacting churches all over to put her on their prayer lists. My mother's name went all the way to India, where a dear pastor resides. He was faithful in including Mom in his personal prayers and also in his staff's daily prayers. There were those who came to Mom's home and not only prayed but put a prayer shawl around her, anointing her and believing God's healing hand to be upon her. These two friends never lost faith in God's healing power for my mother and gave her their prayer shawl as an object of faith. Mom was believing for herself, which prompted us to more faith.

You know how many pray the "no matter what" prayers? Do we really know what we are saying when we pray for God to save, deliver, and heal our loved ones, no matter what? Do we understand that it could cost our loved ones more than we think? I once heard someone declare that they no longer prayed that way; they now pray "with Your love, Lord" or "by Your love Lord, save them." Hmmm, much better, don't you think? I didn't pray a no-matter-what prayer. I stood with boldness, courage, and faith, praying for God's healing hand upon my mother and proclaiming the precious promises of the Word of God!

Dear friends would call or send cards, quoting the scriptures that they were standing on for her healing. Some would tell me, "Sow a seed for her healing." I did all that they suggested and prayed without ceasing for Mom's healing.

Although there were many people of faith praying, claiming the promises of God, another lesson was taught to me through all of this. This was to *know the will of God* when we pray! Inquire of God for *His perfect will* in every situation that we are thrust into. Then prayer can begin, trusting fully in God's answer.

When people questioned why her healing was being postponed, I couldn't answer that until my husband and I went on a three-day fast. We knew God wanted us to anoint her and pray. We didn't know whether the anointing would be for her healing or her burial, but we did it. It was then that we learned it was for her burial, and my husband asked God why. God's response was quick: "Why would you deny Me fellowship with My child?" There were no other words to be spoken after that question from God; we were just to trust Him.

As the cancer and the liver disease progressed, Mom became weary of the fight. She longed to go home, to be with the Lord. This became so evident while I was reading the book *Heaven is for Real*.[3]

CHAPTER 8

Heaven Is Real

Do you know the book entitled *Heaven Is for Real*?[3] Mom wanted so much to read this book, but with her eyes diminishing, she asked if I would read it to her. I enthusiastically agreed, and we would read a section every time we were alone. The story is about three-year old Colton Burpo and his experience in Heaven during surgery.

One day we came to the part when Colton saw his unborn sister in Heaven. Without spoiling the story for you, his mother had a miscarriage but had never discussed it with Colton. Colton met this child while in Heaven. Upon reading this chapter, Mom began to cry and say, "I can't wait!" She repeated it. "I can't wait to see my little girl and Daddy," who had previously passed on.

That is the day I had to stand before my own dear mother and release her. I told her that it was okay to go on to Heaven, made promises to stay close to Dad, and thanked her for being such a selfless mother, a role model to try to replicate. Yes, we cried tears together. But for the most part I stayed strong until I went home. Then I let my guard down and allowed my heart to break, staining my pillow with tears of grief. Though that was hard, today I can allow those days and those moments to heal my heart. I am thankful I had that time with her when we shared what was in our hearts and were able to be so real with one another.

One of the things that ministered most to Mom and me in this book was hearing that Jesus will be the first person we will see when we go to Heaven. As only God can, He confirmed this to me the morning that Mom passed on to Glory. Again God used my loving husband. Within an hour of her passing, my husband was given a vision of Jesus taking Mom into His hands, and he vividly saw Mom's face smiling, asking him to tell all of us to receive the same peace she now had. My beloved husband knelt on his knees in front of my father to tell him the vision. The presence of God fell so intensely that there was a hush that brought the peace of His holiness! To God be the glory!

CHAPTER 9

Tea at 2:00 a.m.

ONE OF THE MOST PRECIOUS STORIES THAT MOM SHARED with me was her 2:00 a.m. tea time with my father. Mom was already bed fast at that time, and she was wide awake in the small hours. Not wanting to wake Dad, she would quietly hum songs. Dad heard her through the monitor he had set up in each of their rooms, and so he went to check on her. Mom sheepishly asked, "What are you doing awake?"

Dad replied, "What are you doing awake?" They both giggled, and Dad inquired whether Mom wanted something to eat or drink.

To his surprise, Mom asked, "Would you mind fixing a cup of tea for me?" Because Mom had not been feeling well enough to eat or drink much and had no particular craving for anything, he happily agreed and went to the kitchen. The words my mother relayed to me about that night still excite me and make me smile. She and Dad reminisced about their life together, expressing gratitude for all the blessings they shared and laughing at all the memories stirring within them. Today I know they had their own tea time with God in those special moments they shared! That night appeared to be a treasure for both of their hearts!

CHAPTER 10

A Sister's Turn

FOR MANY YEARS I WENT WITH MOM AND DAD TO THE family cemeteries. They always reminded me that it would be my duty to care for the plots when they were gone. Therefore, my attending would serve two purposes: one, to remind me how they wanted things done and two, to spend quality time with them. So it was never a drudgery to go on these outings with them. With Mom's sense of humor, she usually made it fun. For instance, one day she chuckled and called me by my two given names. I knew she always meant business then, so I instantly listened. She said, "Now you know, when I'm gone, it will be your job to clean off the bird poop from my headstone." Oh my—only my mother! To this day I still chuckle over her remark, just as she intended.

On one occasion, Mom was too ill to go with Dad and me. On that visit, Dad and I both were having a hard time being there, realizing the diseases were overtaking Mom. We had quite a few graves to clean and arrange flowers for. There were Mom's grandparents, parents, brother, and daughter. As I walked over to my little sister's headstone and began to wipe the dirt off, a boldness came over me, and I started speaking to my sister. "I can't be selfish anymore. It is your turn to be with our mother." I was shocked at the words I was speaking and the love pouring out of my heart. I tell you the truth: when God's spirit lives within you, you may hear things coming out of your mouth that *are* from God, and you are required to heed that voice and those words! Don't understand? One month later my mother passed on. Another lesson learned—take heed of the Holy Spirit! I see this today as God's way of preparing me for the days that were ahead. Take notice of the small things. God is always speaking!

CHAPTER 11

Heeding the Voice of God

EXPERIENCE HAS ALWAYS BEEN THE BEST TEACHER FOR MANY of us. The experience I share now will make all those reading believe in the Holy Spirit, God's voice.

My mother sensed when she would soon be passing on to Heaven, so she heeded the voice of God by preparing two funerals—for her and Dad. Let me share with you about that day. Mom called me at home and said she had cancelled hospice. She wanted me to come down and bring my computer. That was all that she requested, so I hung up the phone, gathered my laptop, and went to their home. When I arrived, she told Dad and me both that we were going to complete pre-need funeral arrangements for the two of them. Dad was against doing any of this, but Mom responded with such tenderness that he sat down beside us and helped with the planning.

I guess by this time I had become numb to my own feelings, knowing that there were things that had to be said and done and just doing them. It wasn't until I left their home, driving the short distance down the road, that the tears began to flow endlessly that day. I decided within me that if Mom could be that strong, then so could I. Her strength empowered me to move forward every day. I could see God in her every moment of her fight. His strength became her strength, His strength became my strength, and so on throughout our family.

The next day Mom went into a coma for the first time. Dad called me and told me that he could not get Mom to wake up. I hung up the phone, called hospice, and then made my way to their house. I found Mom slumped on the couch, unable to move. She was still that way when hospice caregivers came in the door. After checking her vitals, they moved Dad and me to another room, explaining that this was the way it was going to be from now on; she would be sleeping more than she was awake. I began telling the nurse why Mom had cancelled with them the day before, wanting to plan the funerals. The nurse's mouth dropped open, and she said, "She [my mother] knew." Again it was confirmed that Mom had known her time was short. Yet her only thoughts had been towards her family and making things easier for all of us. What love! That's a love that comes straight from God's heart!

CHAPTER 12

A Mother's Sense of Humor

You will really see the sense of humor my mother had with this anecdote. You may recall the pastor and wife I mentioned earlier who were at the hospital when Mom received the grim diagnosis. Well, she purposed in her heart that their next visit would be beneficial to her plans. The day they came, they too had settled in their hearts that this might be their last communal visit with her. However, I'm sure they did not foresee the conversation that ensued.

Mom asked her pastor if he would officiate her funeral. Before he could answer, his wife said, "Are you sure? You know how long-winded he is."

Without hesitation, Mom responded, "I won't mind." That remark lightened the mood and they had a good chuckle.

When things settled down a bit, the pastor answered Mom, saying, "I would be honored."

I pray this dear pastor knows how he honored both our mother and father at their funerals and how much the family sincerely appreciated it. I know how hard it was for him, for all of them were the best of friends. His love for our parents was portrayed in his every word. God bless him!

CHAPTER 13

Angels among Us

Please allow me to share how God's grace encircled my mother before she passed. We all experienced many beautiful moments that we are so thankful for. I now call them "treasured moments of the heart."

A few nights before Mom went to be with the Lord, I was sitting in the living room of her house, by the monitor, where we could hear her. She had been going in and out of a coma by this time, so the monitor allowed us to know when she was awake. I heard her say, "Why won't you talk to me?" There was silence, and then she said, "Huh?" Silence again, before she repeated, "Why won't you talk to me?" A brief silence, and then I heard her voice again. "I know, you are waiting for them to get me all shined up."

I absolutely knew she was seeing an angel, and judging by her questioning, I knew it was not the first time she had seen it. I had been seeing shadows in her room and feeling the presence of the Lord as I prayed over her before and after this event. Is it any wonder that when she drew her last breath there was a smile on her face? Yes, there really was a smile on her face; it was witnessed by family members and hospice staff. How comforting to know that we are never alone! God's Word tells us in Hebrews 13:5[2] that God will "never leave you nor forsake you."

CHAPTER 14

The Hole in My Heart

THE DAY OF MOM'S VIEWING, MY SON CAME TO OUR HOME to check on me. When I looked into his eyes, my own eyes filled with tears. His loving compassion was flowing towards me in such a way that no words were needed. But without hesitation, and with the boldness of the Holy Spirit, words flooded my lips. I responded, "I feel like dancing and praising the Lord, because Mom is in Heaven, with no more pain or sickness—but this hole in my heart will not let me." Since he understood what I was saying, his tight hug was the only comfort I needed at that moment.

I thank God for such loving and compassionate children! The first Christmas without both my parents, they surprised me with a gift more precious than words can express. It was a pillow, made from Dad's shirts, showcasing a picture of Mom and Dad and a poem that reads "This is a shirt I used to wear;

whenever you hold it, know I am there." Now, when that hole in my heart needs to be touched again, I have something tangible to grasp and hold until God's presence lightens my burdens again. I can't thank our children enough for such a sweet gesture!

CHAPTER 15

A Mother's Last Words

AT OUR DEAR MOTHER'S VIEWING, DAD WAS WALKING FROM the casket after his final goodbye. Only the immediate family remained, and we all felt his brokenness as he allowed the tears to fall. Just as he turned away, the lights in the funeral home went out. They didn't just dim—the electricity completely went out.

The funeral home attendant was scurrying to get flashlights for us to see our way out. All the while, she was apologizing and telling us that this had never happened before. She also said that she didn't understand, because the funeral home had two generators to ensure they always had electricity, and these were not coming on. After the attendant searched the surrounding area, she advised us that all the other homes and facilities had electricity; it was just the funeral home that was without power.

At this last comment, we all were looking at each other. We knew it was our dear mother, saying, "That's enough!" This was confirmed when we talked about it later, agreeing that this very thought had been on everyone's mind, knowing Mom's sense of humor. We get it, Mom—you had the last word!

Remembering this moment today reminds me that we need to be prepared for our last word, our last day, our last moment on this earth. For, when the lights go out for us and there is no more power in these fleshly bodies, where will we spend eternity? It is our choice! If we want to spend eternity in Heaven with God the Father, Jesus His Son, and the Holy Spirit, along with many family members and friends, then we must accept Jesus as our Savior and make Him Lord over our lives. It is that simple, asking Him to forgive us of our sins and then believing that Jesus is the Son of God. If you have not done so, do it today, for *today* is the day of Salvation (2 Corinthians 6:2).[2]

CHAPTER 16

A Tribute to Our Mother
(Read at her funeral)

Dear Mom,

When we think of you and your life, we can only hope to be half the person that you were! Throughout our lives, you were there for us. You were the one we turned to in our times of need! You never turned us away but always took the time to give us a listening ear, a shared smile, a hug, and the look of kindness that healed a broken heart. You provided wisdom that we could trust (whether it was hard to hear or confirmed in our hearts).

We have beautiful memories, but the lasting friendship that we shared is a treasure that not only comes from God but also from you! We thank you for the example you were to us. We realize that we are who we are because of your prayers, which covered us all the days of our lives.

We honor you for being the best mother we could have ever had! We thank you for showing family and friends what it means to be a godly woman. And we look forward to seeing you again and never having to say goodbye!

To you Mom, we love you more!

CHAPTER 17

A Husband's Love

1 Corinthians 13[1]

[1]If I had the gift of being able to speak in other languages without learning them and could speak in every language there is in all of heaven and earth, but didn't love others, I would only be making noise. [2]If I had the gift of prophecy and knew all about what is going to happen in the future, knew everything about everything, but didn't love others, what good would it do? Even if I had the gift of faith so that I could speak to a mountain and make it move, I would still be worth nothing at all without love. [3]If I gave everything I have to poor people, and if I were burned alive for preaching the Gospel but didn't love others, it would be of no value whatever. [4]Love is very patient and kind, never jealous or envious, never boastful or proud, [5]never haughty or

selfish or rude. Love does not demand its own way. It is not irritable or touchy. It does not hold grudges and will hardly even notice when others do it wrong. [6] It is never glad about injustice, but rejoices whenever truth wins out. [7] If you love someone, you will be loyal to him no matter what the cost. You will always believe in him, always expect the best of him, and always stand your ground in defending him. [8] All the special gifts and powers from God will someday come to an end, but love goes on forever. Someday prophecy and speaking in unknown languages and special knowledge— these gifts will disappear. [9] Now we know so little, even with our special gifts, and the preaching of those most gifted is still so poor. [10] But when we have been made perfect and complete, then the need for these inadequate special gifts will come to an end, and they will disappear. [11] It's like this: when I was a child I spoke and thought and reasoned as a child does. But when I became a man my thoughts grew far beyond those of my childhood, and now I have put away the childish things. [12] In the same way, we can see and understand only a little about God now, as if we were peering at his reflection in a poor mirror; but someday we are going to see him in his completeness, face-to-face. Now all that I know is hazy and blurred, but then I will see everything clearly, just as clearly as God sees into my heart right now.

[13] There are three things that remain—faith, hope, and love—and the greatest of these is love.

This scripture defines the love between my mother and my father. During Mom's illness, my father was admitted to the hospital for pneumonia, and he had a heart attack during his stay. He was transported to another hospital two hours away for the heart issue. Yet his only worry was his dear wife. His only desire was to get back to her quickly. My siblings and I were taking care of Mom and spending time with Dad at the hospital, but in Dad's eyes no one was going to care for her as he would. Thus he was anxious to get back home to her. That's love!

Over the years, Dad had been diagnosed with several diseases, and he was being treated by different doctors. However, after Mom's passing he only wanted to go be with her in Heaven; he was tiring of all the doctors' visits and all the medication. Those who knew my dad would agree that part of him was missing after Mom went to Heaven. Thankfully, family and close friends gave Dad the stamina and courage to fight his diseases and depression during this time. He would always become enthusiastic when telling me about a visit or a phone call. He loved family and friends with a deepness that cannot be expressed. Then God blessed him with a great-granddaughter, and his disposition rose to a new level when that little one came to visit. To see his smile when this precious baby girl grinned at him still warms my heart when I think of it today. Thank God for the sweet memories—more "treasures of the heart"!

My parents shared a unique love. We knew that Dad would never replace Mom with another, even though we encouraged him to do so. When we were growing up, the vehicles had a full seat across the front so Mom would always be in the middle, by Dad's side. They were always touching one another; they never walked anywhere without holding each other's hand.

Dad always referred to Mom as "honey"—and two grandchildren thought that was her name! Dad and Mom were elated that those two grandchildren lovingly called them Paw and Honey, even throughout their adult years.

God's Hand of Mercy

NOW TO TELL YOU OF THE MIRACLE THAT MY FATHER received. Dad had started declining in health, and one day was having trouble breathing and was experiencing chest pain, so he agreed to go to the emergency room. The ER doctor pronounced, "The test results show that you have lung cancer. You are a very sick man. I'm worried about you. Call your doctor first thing in the morning." He walked out of the room and left Dad and me with our eyes locked on each other, no words being expressed. Talk about being hit by a brick! We did not get a chance to ask any questions. We heard the doctor's opinion, and that was that.

My mind was racing. Yes, without God, there seemed to be no hope. Scripture started bombarding my mind like a freight train: "But, there is a God whose ways are higher than ours, His thoughts are higher than ours." (Isaiah 55:9).[2] "But, with God, all things are possible" (Matthew 19:26).[2]

With these words forming inside of me, my faith was rising to yet another challenge, and I said, "Well, God, I'm trusting You again! No matter what, You are still God!"

A few days passed, and on to the pulmonary doctor we went, to review the x-ray results from the hospital where Dad had been diagnosed with inoperable lung cancer. After much discussion, Dad advised the doctor that he did not want any treatments or biopsies. His desire was only to be kept comfortable when the time came. Dad's reasoning came from seeing his siblings and his wife dying of cancer and realizing that those who endured the radiation and chemotherapy did no better than those who chose not to do any treatments. The doctor was very kind and considerate of Dad's feelings. He encouraged us to go and do now whatever we wanted to do, and added, "Make as many memories as you can." Once again I found myself sitting with a parent and discussing hospice, with no hope being verbalized from the doctor. Of course my mind was flooded with memories of the same scenario that had transpired with my mother, and I remembered that two months after she'd been told the same thing she was gone. Yet again, I had to fight my emotions and be strong for a parent as we walked out of that office. Remembering the lesson I'd learned going through this with my mother, I got in the car and quietly asked God, "Father God, this is man's prognosis. What is Yours?"

Very softly, He replied, "He is in line for a miracle." My entire attitude changed with those few words. As it happened, I was going to the "Night of Miracles" that evening at our local church! This was a night set aside for prayer, fasting, and revival. After the sermon, an altar call was given, and many went forward for prayer. Then it happened. The man of God stopped praying for people in the prayer line and walked to the microphone to say, "God has dropped one word into my spirit—cancer." I knew God was doing His thing, so I took that walk of faith to stand in the gap for my father! All I remember as the preacher touched my head to pray for me was that I kept saying, "Enough is enough"—and in my mind I started stomping the devil under my feet.

CHAPTER 19

The Ride in Daytona

WITHIN ONE MONTH, DAD WAS WELL ENOUGH TO GO TO Florida and ride in Dale Earnhardt's car at 170 mph, at Daytona Raceway with my siblings! My sister explains it this way: "My biggest memory is that smile on his face that never left! We were so worried if he would be able to get in and out of the car, and he jumped out of it like a ten-year-old—a lot better than the rest of us!"

That ride was a dream come true, for NASCAR was a true passion of both my parents. While we were growing up, NASCAR was a fixture on our television every week during its season. Later in their years, our mom and dad were blessed to go to a Daytona race for their anniversary. Their eyes were flooded with love and their voices with excitement as they told of their adventure. Oh, how thankful they were to experience such a venture and how thankful we were for them to do so, and now we have treasures of the heart!

On Dad's next trip back to the doctor, he was told that there was no change—*no progression!*—in the mass that was attached to both lungs. It was our answer to prayer. He was in line for a miracle!

What did that ride in Daytona do for Dad? Sitting with the pulmonary doctor that day, he was oblivious to the good news he'd just heard about no progression. He was enthusiastically telling the doctor all about his experience in Daytona. I remember the doctor smiling as he looked over at me and gave me a wink. He was reminding me of his previous instructions to do everything we wanted to do with Dad now. For months, Dad kept experiencing the thrill of Daytona by recalling the details every time he could. What a blessing!

CHAPTER 20

He Will Live and Not Die

Ten months after the initial diagnosis, on a routine doctor visit, we were told that the mass in Dad's lungs might be growing. The doctor also advised that another mass was forming in the bottom of one lung.

Dad was seriously ill at this point, and we began getting help with him from hospice. He loved his nurse and aide; he felt comfortable with them. Because we had hospice help before, I knew that he would have the chance to talk to them about concerns and choices that he didn't feel comfortable enough to discuss with his children. So we always left it up to him whether he wanted us there when hospice workers arrived.

If you have already lost a loved one, you know how hard it can be to sit and try to be encouraging or just to listen to what is in the person's heart. As a caregiver, you have the same hurts and pain in knowing that time is short.

Sometimes it was so painful to be with Dad that it felt like my heart was breaking into pieces. (Did I mention that I am a Daddy's girl?) But I knew that God would give me the strength to carry on, just as He did with my dear mother.

One Sunday evening I went to visit Dad, and while he was talking, I heard the Holy Spirit whisper, "He will live and not die." I knew what He was saying, because our pastor had just that morning preached a sermon entitled "I Will Live and Not Die"! The message was regarding the promises of God and expounding on the fact that when we are children of God, we will not experience death but be led straight into Heaven. In reminiscing on the sermon, I heard the same words again: "He will live and not die." At that moment I realized, *Yes, if Dad does not get his physical healing on this earth, he will indeed be made whole when he joins Heaven.* There was a leap of joy in my heart just knowing that my father was saved. He was a child of the King, so yes, he would join our Heavenly Father, and his precious wife, when his time came to pass from this earth.

When Dad did pass on to Heaven, it had been one year since his diagnosis of lung cancer, and *that*, my friend, *is* a miracle for that disease! Yet the biggest miracle (and gift for all of us) is salvation—spending eternity with God! I thank you, Father God, that Dad made that decision when he was young and lived the example of the Christian life throughout his years! What a tremendous blessing for us, his family!

CHAPTER 21

God Always Prepares the Way

ONE OF DAD'S GRANDCHILDREN HAD A DREAM THE NIGHT before he passed into glory. She dismissed the dream the next morning, believing it was because she had been talking to me before retiring to sleep. We had been discussing how much time hospice staff believed we had left with my dad and I responded with their answer that day—two months.

In this dream, the grandchild was making her way to visit her grandfather and was extremely surprised to find her grandmother (who had already passed on to Heaven) opening the door for her. At once this grandchild heard herself saying, "He will be with you soon." The next day, Dad was gone.

I believe this grandchild has inherited the same gifts her grandmother had, so I am encouraging her to heed the voice of God as she learns more about Him and the operation of His gifts. To God be the Glory!

CHAPTER 22

Be Like Thumper

Let us be like Thumper, the rabbit—if you do not have anything nice to say, do not say anything at all. I'm still amazed at how cruel some people can be at the worst time in others' lives. I would like to believe things are said because the person does not know what to say. But since they are still strangers to us, I cannot comment on the reason why they say such things.

This story takes place at our father's funeral viewing. Amid our receiving numerous compliments and stories about our father's character, a lady walked up to one of my siblings and proclaimed, "Well, I guess you are an orphan now." How do you respond to that? The person who spoke it was even a stranger to my sibling; they had no idea who she was.

Well, to that stranger I respond, "No, we are not! Our Father, who resides in Heaven, is the creator of *all* humanity.

He knows every hair on our heads, and He loves us so much that He sent His Only Son to the cross to die in our place. Now we can live and not die! We can step into Glory to meet our earthly parents again, to *live* with them for evermore! Thank you for reminding us of this, my dear stranger."

CHAPTER 23

Celebrating Life

WITH ANY FUNERAL, IF YOU KNOW WHERE YOUR FRIEND OR loved one is going upon the natural death, it dictates whether you can truly celebrate his or her life. As for my parents, we know they are with God in Heaven for eternity, so we celebrated them.

Those not believing in Jesus as the Son of God nor inviting Him to be a part of their lives have no hope of seeing their loved one again. They only experience the pain of their loss, with no peace or comfort.

After my father's funeral, someone knocked on my vehicle window, prompting me to roll it down. I did not know the person; she introduced herself as a longtime friend of both my parents. Her next words have stayed with me, and she will never know how much it still blesses me to think upon them. In consoling me, she said, "I loved the service. It was more like a revival than a funeral, a true celebration of his life." Her words penetrated my heart, for the entire service had been dedicated to Dad as a "legacy of love"!

Thank You, God, that we could celebrate our parents' lives and not mourn their eternal destruction!

CHAPTER 24

A Tribute to Our Father
(Read at his funeral)

TO OUR DEAR DAD, WHO WILL REMAIN OUR HERO FOREVER in our hearts.

You could not have been a better father to us! The examples you set and the lessons that you taught us make us want to be "just like Dad."

Your soft-spoken voice and the love behind each word takes sincerity to the highest level. A niece said it best when she said, "Your dad was so gentle, but underneath he was so strong."

Your family always came first to you, Dad, and we saw this in all you did. The integrity you portrayed was exceptional too, whether on the job or with friends and family. Your word was your word, and you would do everything in your power to ensure it remained so.

You always had a way to make our extended family and friends feel welcome and loved. We have received so many compliments about you through the years that time will not allow us to share here. So just know, Dad, how loved you really are and that you will remain in our hearts forever!

One last thing, our dear father. *Thank you* for being the loving husband you were to our sweet mother! You showed us what true love is between a man and a woman, setting the example not just for us but for all those who knew you. You took care of Mom in such a loving way and gave her your best in caring for her the last years of her life. Your love can be summarized with words from a friend: "From one short visit in their home, it was evident that they loved one another very much."

We love you, Dad, and will never forget that you are leaving us with a wonderful legacy, the legacy of love!

CHAPTER 25

No Regrets

I WANT TO ENCOURAGE EVERY READER TO LIVE WITH *NO regrets*. We all have been told to love, spend quality time with, communicate with, and show respect, etc. for all people; then we will have no regrets. However, the duties of life always seem to interfere, causing us heartache when we wonder, "If I had only ..."

I had one of those moments after the passing of my mother, and the thought hindered me for months. I was finally able to let it go when I sat in a prayer service and the pianist started playing one of the songs that Mom and I had shared together. Rushing through my mind was a memory of a day that Mom asked me to play the piano for her. At that point, she was unable to do anything more than be moved from the bed to a chair. I refused her request, not wanting her to hear how much skill I had lost by not playing the piano for years.

Understandably, she persisted, but to no avail. I still refused; I regretted that I had not continued playing for my own benefit. After all, I had only been five years old at my first recital. I had not had much of a choice back then, since my mother had been the piano teacher. But why hadn't I honored her request that day? I knew that God would have honored me and that no matter what I heard in the natural world, Mom would have heard a sweet sound from Heaven. But I allowed fear and the spirit of rejection to take over my mind. Nevertheless, when this memory popped into my mind that day, I allowed God to take it from me, healing the brokenness that I brought to Him. If this story has prompted you, the reader, to remember moments in your life of such regret, may you turn them into lessons instead of regret.

This is to show you that in the loss of someone dear there should not be regret on our part for anything. For this is what I learned after the passing of my parents. Both times, I was regretting things I had done or not done for them. I felt that if I could have one more day, I could rectify my feelings. But God reminded me that there are no more tears, no more sorrow in Heaven (Revelation 21:4), so our loved ones are no longer remembering the things that I was burdened with.

Therefore, take heart my dear family and friends! Let your hearts heal completely from the unsettled situations you are holding onto. The only thing our loved ones know now is joy, and it is joy unspeakable and full of glory!

Psalm 16:11[2] tells us, "In Your [God's] presence is fullness of joy."

CHAPTER 26

Circle of Love

As I sit with a cup of tea today, glorying in God's holy presence, I want to pass on to my family what my parents and grandparents instilled in me. Their prayers are still being answered today for their family. Please know that when I am no longer on this earth, my prayers for you will continue throughout the ages also. Prayers don't end with the passing of a person; God is continually sending forth the answers to our prayers. Never despair that you do not see the answers in your time. God has His perfect timing; our job is to trust it.

Our family was blessed with a magnitude of love! I could not begin to explain all the memories I have of our parents and grandparents showing their love to their family. They genuinely acknowledged each family member as if he or she were the only one in their lives when they spent time with them. The sacrificing I witnessed is invaluable to me now. It is a reminder of what true love is, for there was no selfishness portrayed in their acts of kindness to and for each family member. I also witnessed their love and kindness being extended to friends and acquaintances throughout their years; they were treated as immediate family. They truly represented God's hands being extended, no matter what the need. Then there were the strangers who found their way to my grandparents' house, needing food. Our grandparents' home was set along the main road, so hobos (as they were called in that day) found their way there, and Grandma never let them continue their journeys without full stomachs. Hebrews 13:2[1] says, "Don't forget to be kind to strangers, for some who have done this have entertained angels without realizing it!" My parents and grandparents always set the example of loving their neighbors, as specified in Mark 12:30–32.

Thankfully, this love I'm discussing continues through generations, because we witnessed how to treat others. I want to express my gratitude for some special cousins that I was blessed to grow up with. Our families were always together and had many sleepovers. Various reasons prompted this, from our parents enjoying one another's company into the wee hours of the morning to the times my aunt and uncle kept me and my siblings overnight due to my baby sister being rushed to the hospital. We shared many beautiful memories together and, yes, got into some orneriness too. But these cousins were always there in time of need, even though miles separated us as we grew older. They provided dinners for both my parents' funerals, and their thoughtfulness and generosity are forever etched into my mind and heart. Their parents taught them selfless love also, and they put it into action for us. Because they live their lives this way for many, they may not realize that the essence of their acts of kindness shows all people that they are in contact with the ministry of Christianity: J-O-Y.

J = Jesus; O = Others; Y = You

May God bless each one of them with His abundance, as only He can!

All families have their ups and downs, and ours have not been exempt. However, the bond of love continually helps us to overlook our weaknesses, failures, and hurts. It allows us to forgive one another freely. Yes, we are human, so it may take us a while to get over certain things, but there is no doubt that we will. A sign hanging in my home reads, "Family—forever, for always, no matter what." It's a good reminder for all of us. Agape love (sacrificial love) can only come from God. His love enables us to treat one another correctly. 1 Peter 4:8[1] says, "Most important of all, continue to show deep love for each other, for love makes up for many of your faults."

There will be a day when we can all stand in a circle of love again. We must not let the circle be broken by a missing piece. Let us realize God's love for all of us today. Total surrender to God enables Him to remove all of our pain, healing our brokenness and giving us hope. He helps us to forgive and forget, to let it all go and leave it in His hands. God can restore and will give us double for our trouble (Isaiah 61:7).[2]

One day I visited my grandmother in the nursing home where she was transitioning from this life to Heaven, under the care of hospice. It came as no surprise that memories were flooding my soul. In the stillness of those moments, I began thinking of the many rewards that our parents and grandparents will reap with joy as they enter Heaven's gates. My heart started shouting, "Won't it be glorious over there!" When the time approached for us to leave, my husband and I anointed her and prayed for Grandma to have complete peace and comfort through her transition.

It was then I heard so softly from God's Holy Spirit: "The best days in the natural may be behind us, but the best days in the supernatural are yet ahead!"

My only response was, "So be it, Lord Jesus!" She did pass peacefully, as many had prayed for her to. At the funeral, two grandsons ministered to our families with beautiful and sweet memories of Grandma in their eulogies. Although tears of grief were shed, there were also moments of laughter upon hearing about the orneriness of the grandchildren. One grandson told about a picture of Jesus hanging in our grandparents' home. Grandma had never failed to remind this grandson that Jesus was watching what he was doing and was going to come down and get him if he didn't act right. That grandson didn't tell us whether that changed his behavior or not at the time. However, it did leave an impact on his life.

The pastor who presided over Grandma's service read Proverbs 31, depicting her in this scripture. It touched my heart tremendously, as I had used this scripture to refer to my mother in this book. I kept reiterating "Like mother, like daughter" in my mind.

As I drink another cup of tea, I reminisce on all of this. I find that my goal is to do the same as my parents and grandparents did—to share love and joy with all people that

God puts in my path. I pray that through this book God will give hope to the hearts that are broken, love to those who feel rejection, peace for the ones filled with anxiety, and comfort to those who are grief-stricken. I absolutely know that with one word from your mouth to God's ears, it can all be healed and restored. That word is *Jesus*!

CHAPTER 27

God's Protection

THE NAME JESUS IS WITHOUT A DOUBT ANYTHING WE NEED IT to be. One story that remains in my mind is about protection. I learned very quickly that day that if there is no time to pray, protection can be found in the name *Jesus*. Our family was traveling by car and running late. Midway into our trip I was impressed to pray. I closed my eyes and started to silently pray. As I did, I was given a vision of us passing a car on a straight piece of road, but as we were passing the car, we collided. I immediately started praying against that crash, using the name of Jesus. I was still praying when I felt our car speed up and begin to pass the one in front of us. I opened my eyes to vividly see the crash again and hear tires squealing. I screamed "Jesus!"—and, as if in slow motion, our cars intertwined and went through one another. The next thing we knew we were in front of the other car, on the correct side of the road, as if nothing had happened.

Have you ever been traveling down a road in a terrible rainstorm, finding it hard to see, and suddenly your car started hydroplaning? This happened to me once while I was traveling for work. To make matters worse, it was dark, and I was in unknown territory. I found my car headed for the cement wall of a bridge just ahead of me. All I could do was scream out "Jesus!" The steering wheel turned and straightened the car, carrying me across the bridge and on to the other side.

My husband and I had another experience that neither of us will ever forget, for there was a lesson born of it too. After being on top of a mountain, overlooking God's beautiful creation, we got into our SUV and proceeded down the mountain. We were praying for our children, and we ended the prayer as we always do, "In the name of Jesus, amen." I had started taking pictures with my camera outside of the side window, when suddenly I felt something hit my hand, and I jerked it back inside. The hit was hard enough to knock the batteries out of the camera. At that moment, the instruments on the SUV started sounding and flashing. We found ourselves with no brakes or power steering. While my husband was using the emergency brake to try to slow the vehicle down, I was screaming "Jesus!" while fear penetrated my heart. The road was nothing but S-curves and straight drops to the side. I cannot tell you how many miles my husband fought that emergency brake and steering wheel, but all the while my prayers for protection and rebuking of Satan continued. We were able to get to the bottom of that mountain, and later, when I had the pictures developed, we found one that we did not understand at first. We enlarged the photo to clarify what we were seeing. It was a rope connected to the front of the SUV on the passenger's side, going up above the top of the SUV. We have had many people look at this photo, and they all see the same thing. Of course, in our infinite minds, we were blaming the devil for wreaking havoc. Then my husband heard God inquire, "How do you know that I didn't send you that rope to hold you back?" What was our lesson? It was to see God's hand at work in all our situations, not to look for or dwell on the negative!

God has worked His miracle working power in other ways than protection from car accidents. When our son was a sixteen-month-old toddler, he fell from a two-story window when he leaned against a loose screen. My heart was beating out of my chest when I went to get him. There was blood coming out of his mouth, but he was awake and crying. I loaded him in the car and headed to the local hospital, where they pronounced that he had a laceration inside his mouth, but it was not deep enough to stitch. He had no broken bones or internal bleeding. Thank God!

I have had many friends express similar situations that they and their family members have experienced. But their stories are their own to share. I am extremely grateful for the faith my parents, grandparents, many relatives, and close friends have instilled in me; they have encouraged me to go deeper with God for myself. I pray these stories will validate who God is, or can be, in your life.

The moral of these stories and others like them - God took care of the situations supernaturally! We don't need to know whether He sent a band of angels or descended His hand from Heaven—we just know *He* did it. We must never despise the name of Jesus! He gave His life for ours. We can ask God for anything in the name of Jesus, and it will be done, according to His Will.

Speaking God's Word (the Bible) brings it to life. One story will demonstrate what I mean by this remark. My husband's grandmother was in the hospital and not expected to make it through the night. My husband decided to sit with her all night, pray, and read the Word to her. The next morning his grandmother woke up as if nothing was wrong. She ate ice cream, talked about family memories, and was clear and concise in her mind. But a few days later, she went to Heaven. When my husband inquired with God what that was about, God responded with, "How could I not have allowed her back, due to all the Word spoken over her?" Our lesson here? We can prolong death for our loved ones, but we cannot stop it.

Read the Book of Acts for all that is done in the name of Jesus and the will of God.

CHAPTER 28

God's Love

John 3:16–17[1] says, "[16] For God loved the world so much that he gave his only Son so that anyone who believes in him shall not perish but have eternal life. [17] God did not send his Son into the world to condemn it, but to save it."

Romans 8:38–39[1] tells us about the depth of God's love for each of us. It reads "[38] For I am convinced that nothing can ever separate us from his love. Death can't, and life can't. The angels won't, and all the powers of hell itself cannot keep God's love away. Our fears for today, our worries about tomorrow, [39] or where we are—high above the sky, or in the deepest ocean— nothing will ever be able to separate us from the love of God demonstrated by our Lord Jesus Christ when he died for us."

God has shown us His love in such a way that it is truly amazing to me. Think about it. Do you love the people of this world so much that you are willing to give your own life, or that of a child, for even one other person? Many of us would agree that to save one of our children from disease or destruction, we could easily say yes to giving up our own lives. But as to giving up my child for a stranger, I cannot fathom that situation. Yet, God did that for you and me. He gave Jesus to die in our place that we may live!

Numerous times throughout the years I have been on a cruise ship, calmly standing in a lineup and being instructed what to do in case of an emergency. I absolutely know there would not be any kind of calmness among the passengers in a real emergency. There would be nothing but chaos, and many would be pushing and shoving to get to those lifeboats. Their motto would be "Every man for himself." So, each time I stand there, I set the purpose in my heart that I would be one of the last to leave. This is because I know that Heaven is my home, and I can't wait to get there. As I scan the crowd around me, I assume that there are those who have not made the decision to follow Christ, and this would give them another opportunity to do so.

Now, before you say I'm judging, please know that the Word tells us we will know them by their fruit (Matthew 7:20). What I know is that eternity is so long that our infinite minds cannot fathom its existence. I do not hate anyone enough to hope they spend eternity in hell. People who make the comment that they "live in hell" do not comprehend what a real and living hell encompasses. The torture is unbearable and something that I wish not to write about. Are you wondering how I know this? I know firsthand that hell is real. I inquired of God to show me whether one of my relatives had gone to Heaven or hell, and I still get emotional when I remember how He showed me the truth. As I walked up to the casket at the viewing, I could only see the face of my relative, with flames of fire rising to the top of his neck. I saw him screaming at me, "Tell them the truth! Tell them the truth!" So, my dear loved ones and dear friends, I plead with you today to refuse hell and choose Jesus Christ as your Savior. Jesus remains your Way, Truth, and Life, your only way to Father God and an eternal Heaven! Ultimately, the choice is yours to make. If I could make it for you, I would make Heaven your home. The torment of hell is for eternity. We can't wrap our minds around that word, *eternity*, for our life is but a vapor (James 4:14).[2]

God wants us to receive an agape love from Him so that we can freely give that love to others. Although I'm still a work in progress, in God's eyes that's okay, as long as I lean on Him for guidance and direction. I love what a footnote in TLB version says. It alludes to us not necessarily dying in someone else's place but being ready to listen, help, encourage, and give to others. We should give all the love we can and then give a little more. I pray to be readily available when God calls me to a task, for I know the task will show the love of Christ through me. I'm extremely thankful to God and Jesus Christ His Son, that they bore that cross for me so I would not need to! That is undeniable love, compassion, mercy, and grace bestowed to all of us who will receive!

I recently called a friend to give my regards and sympathy in the loss of her mother. But I was the one who was blessed during our conversation. This was part of her comment to me: "There is peace in knowing she's in a better place with her loved ones whom she's been longing to see—and Jesus! You are right about spending those last hours with her. I'm so thankful I got to be there. The song that goes 'On a day like today, when my Jesus I shall see … what a glorious day that will be' came to my mind and hasn't left. Praise God, her struggle is over. Victory is won. I'll miss her terribly, but I must strive to join her."

I was just following Galatians 6:2[2], "Bear one another's burdens, and so fulfill the law of Christ" when I attempted to comfort my friend, but her response was healing to my heart also. I believe that is why God instructs us not to forsake the fellowship of other believers, for we all benefit from it. God's love, God's presence, and God's anointing are not only precious but healing, comforting, and life-changing. Whatever we need, we get.

I hear this question asked many times: "Why can't everyone let others alone and let them just live their lives?" This is why I can't—allowing a sinner to stay in sin without telling him the truth of God's Word and how to make Heaven his home leads to him spending eternity in hell. Speaking truth to that person allows him to make the choice for himself.

If you are reading this, you still have time to make the correct choice. Choose eternal life! Jesus wants you to come to Him as you are; you don't need to clean yourself up before coming to Him. He paid the price for you when He went to the cross. Jesus is waiting for you today!

It doesn't take special language. Prayer is just talking to our Heavenly Father. You just need to believe that Jesus is the Son of God. John 14:6[1] tells us, "Jesus told him, 'I am the Way—yes, and the Truth and the Life. No one can get to the Father except by means of Me.'" Repent of your sins and ask Jesus to live in your heart. When you do this, God's Holy Spirit will guide you into a better life, one that ends with eternal life in Heaven. Salvation is a gift from God (Ephesians 2:8).[1]

CHAPTER 29

The True Work of Love

SOME BELIEVERS ARE NOT ACTING OUT THE TRUE WORK OF love, which is reconciliation. Reconciling means to cause to be friendly or harmonious again; to adjust, to settle differences. Often, as Christians, we are too judgmental. If we would only realize that we cannot detect the depth of pain in others. If we could, we would have more empathy toward them. Since we only see the outward show of their pain in drugs, alcohol, abuse, or even cutting, we need to understand that they are using these devices to cover their pain. When I feel the walls closing in on me and I am filled with anxiety, I too, sometimes feel tempted to numb my emotions. However, I have God's Holy Spirit living inside me, which is greater than any temptation that comes at me. With prayer, I can walk away from those vices. When we help others, love always prevails, so we must show love freely.

For too many years I judged and criticized people because I had a religious spirit. Aside from numerous teachings that caused this, I didn't like myself and was always trying to be and do better. One day I had an epiphany that set me free. I saw that I was doing this because I was dwelling on the negative, seeing no positive aspects within myself. I was always striving for perfection, believing that was what God demanded, for many around me expected it. Then, when I allowed God to show His love to me and I studied about His love in His Word, I was able to declare Him my loving Father and not just the disciplinarian I had seen Him as. With that new outlook, I was able to allow His love to flow freely through me to others. That is what changed me so that I looked for the best in others.

With Jesus in your heart, it is much easier to show mercy to those who need it. For clarification, read Romans 8 and allow His truth to enter your heart too.

It still bothers me today to know how many people I have hurt over the years with my words and actions. Even when God leads me to apologize, the only way I can move on is to pray that God turns all their hurt into good for them (Romans 8:28). I see now that I usually reacted out of pain—being wounded and broken myself, I needed inner healing. I try harder now not to react based on my feelings. I try not to allow my situation to dictate my actions. I try to take notice and understand why some people act as they do; their hurt can be so deep that they are reacting from *their* place of pain also. All addictive behavior is used to cover deeper pain. Hurtful situations cause us to revert back to whatever covers the pain. My husband and I have counseled all ages for many things, including drug and alcohol abuse, pornography, marital problems, childhood abuse, domestic abuse, and sadly, "cutting." One thing we found is this: Without God, they were never delivered from the problem.

As I write this, my mind rushes from my husband and children, to parents and siblings, to family and friends, and to church members whom I have hurt. I learned many lessons in hardship and hurt feelings. But God—God forgives and restores! With tremendous gratitude I can speak to God, as I do to my husband and children, saying, "Thank you for loving me in spite of."

CHAPTER 30

The Good News

I ASKED A FEW FRIENDS TO PRAY FOR ME AS I BEGAN THIS endeavor of writing a book. When I thought the book was at completion, one of those friends sent me this message. It is the reason that I'm writing these last chapters. The message was as follows:

Hey, Debi! How are things going with your book? I was praying for you today and had a vision that I wanted to share. I saw two women, in what looked to be a bookstore, fighting over a book with your name as the author. The bookstore looked to be rioted or in disrepair. I could hear one of the women say, "I need this for my family. It will tell us what happened!" I believe your book is going to be an asset after the Rapture for those who are left behind. Those who will be searching for the truth and are willing to give their lives for

Christ during the tribulation will be using your book as one of their greatest tools.

I wish to leave no stone unturned. I hope to guide every unbeliever onto the path of Jesus Christ, the Savior of the world. I pray that the pessimist will see the truth of God's Word and not have any more doubt within his heart or negativity in his communication. I will be quoting numerous scriptures in these chapters so that God Himself will be the truth bearer!

We are to love God with all our heart and soul and mind and strength. (Mark 12:30[1]). Acts 16:31[1] tells us to "Believe on the Lord Jesus Christ and you will be saved."

Everywhere Jesus preached, He called the people to repentance. See Matthew 4:17; Matthew 9:13; and Luke 13:3, where He told the Galileans, "I tell you … unless you repent you will all likewise perish."

The meaning of the word *repent* in the *Merriam-Webster's Collegiate Dictionary* is "to turn from sin and resolve to reform one's life; to feel sorry for something done; regret." I heard one pastor easily clarify the word *repent* by saying, "change direction." That is what it entails; to repent of our sins is to go in another direction. To stay the same course would keep us in our sins.

Second Corinthians 7:10[2] tells us that "Godly sorrow produces repentance leading to salvation." True sorrow leads to tears of repentance, which prompt us to want to change.

Once we have repented of our sins, God remembers them no more! How thankful we should be for an omnipotent (almighty, all-powerful, invincible, supreme) and merciful God such as He!

Hebrews 8:12[2] explains, "For I will be merciful to their unrighteousness, and their sins and their lawless deeds I will remember no more."

That is all there is to do on our part. But it is so rewarding to begin an intimate relationship with God, our Father; Jesus, His Son; and His Holy Spirit, by praying and reading His Word. We get to know their characters and attributes by reading the Word, and it changes us into their likeness.

I need God's wisdom, knowledge, understanding, guidance, mercy, grace, and love to lead me daily. In taking the time to read God's Word, inevitably, sometime throughout my day, I will be reminded of a scripture that I need to stand on. Sometimes it is just a reminder to not take offense; other times it reminds me to love and forgive those who are trying to hurt me or a loved one. The Word of God will always point us in the correct direction.

In the Bible, two men of God clearly spoke the fullness of the gospel—which means "good news." It can be read in its entirety. Stephen's testimony is found in Acts 7:2–53, and Paul addressed the Jews in Acts 13:16–43. I encourage you to read this to help you understand the life of Jesus Christ.

Colossians 1:20–25[1]

[20] It was through what his Son did that God cleared a path for everything to come to him—all things in Heaven and on earth—for Christ's death on the cross has made peace

with God for all by his blood. [21] This includes you who were once so far away from God. You were his enemies and hated him and were separated from him by your evil thoughts and actions, yet now he has brought you back as his friends. [22] He has done this through the death on the cross of his own human body, and now as a result Christ has brought you into the very presence of God, and you are standing there before him with nothing left against you—nothing left that he could even chide you for; [23] the only condition is that you fully believe the Truth, standing in it steadfast and firm, strong in the Lord, convinced of the Good News that Jesus died for you, and never shifting from trusting him to save you. This is the wonderful news that came to each of you and is now spreading all over the world …

Philippians 1:6[1]

And I am sure that God who began the good work within you will keep right on helping you grow in his grace until his task within you is finally finished on that day when Jesus Christ returns.

Jeremiah 29:11[1]

For I know the plans I have for you, says the Lord. They are plans for good and not for evil, to give you a future and a hope.

1 Peter 1:2–25[1]

[2] Dear friends, God the Father chose you long ago and

knew you would become his children. And the Holy Spirit has been at work in your hearts, cleansing you with the blood of Jesus Christ and making you to please him. May God bless you richly and grant you increasing freedom from all anxiety and fear. ³ All honor to God, the God and Father of our Lord Jesus Christ; for it is his boundless mercy that has given us the privilege of being born again so that we are now members of God's own family. Now we live in the hope of eternal life because Christ rose again from the dead. ⁴ And God has reserved for his children the priceless gift of eternal life; it is kept in Heaven for you, pure and undefiled, beyond the reach of change and decay. ⁵ And God, in his mighty power, will make sure that you get there safely to receive it because you are trusting him. It will be yours in that coming last day for all to see. ⁶ So be truly glad! There is wonderful joy ahead, even though the going is rough for a while down here. ⁷ These trials are only to test your faith, to see whether or not it is strong and pure. It is being tested as fire tests gold and purifies it—and your faith is far more precious to God than mere gold; so if your faith remains strong after being tried in the test tube of fiery trials, it will bring you much praise and glory and honor on the day of his return. ⁸ You love him even though you have never seen him; though not seeing him, you trust him; and even now you are happy with the inexpressible joy that comes from Heaven itself. ⁹ And your further reward for trusting him will be the salvation of your souls. ¹⁰ This salvation was something the prophets did not fully understand. Though they wrote about it, they had many questions as to what it all could mean.¹¹ They wondered what the Spirit of Christ within them was talking about, for he told them to write down the events which, since then, have happened to Christ: his suffering and his great glory afterwards. And they wondered when and to whom all this would happen. ¹² They were finally told that these things would not occur during their lifetime but long years later, during yours. And now at last this Good News has been plainly announced to all of us. It was preached to us in the power of the same Heaven-sent Holy Spirit who spoke to them; and it is all so strange and wonderful that even the angels in Heaven would give a great deal to know more about it. ¹³ So now you can look forward soberly and intelligently to more of God's kindness to you when Jesus Christ returns. ¹⁴ Obey God because you are his children; don't slip back into your old ways—doing evil because you knew no better. ¹⁵ But be holy now in everything you do, just as the Lord is holy, who invited you to be his child. ¹⁶ He himself has said, "You must be holy, for I am holy." ¹⁷ And remember that your Heavenly Father to whom you pray has no favorites when he judges. He will judge you with perfect justice for everything you do; so act in reverent fear of him from now on until you get to Heaven. ¹⁸ God paid a ransom to save you from the impossible road to Heaven which your fathers tried to take, and the ransom he paid was not mere gold or silver as you very well know. ¹⁹ But he paid for you with the precious lifeblood of Christ, the sinless, spotless Lamb of God. ²⁰ God chose him for this purpose long before the world began, but only recently was he brought into public view, in these last days, as a blessing to you. ²¹ Because of this, your trust can be in God who raised Christ from the dead and gave him great glory. Now your faith and hope can rest in him alone. ²² Now you can have real love for everyone because your souls have been cleansed from selfishness and hatred when you trusted Christ to save you; so see to it that you really do love each other warmly, with all your hearts. [23] For you have a new life. It was not passed on to you from your parents, for the life they gave you will fade away. This new one will last forever, for it comes from Christ, God's ever-living Message to men. [24] Yes, our natural lives will fade as grass does when it becomes all brown and dry. All our greatness is like a flower that droops and falls; [25] but the Word of the Lord will last forever. And his message is the Good News that was preached to you.

CHAPTER 31

Remain Watchful

I'M GOING TO SOUND THE ALARM FOR OUR NEED TO REMAIN watchful and prepared for His Coming. In Mark 13, Jesus tells us about remaining watchful.

Mark 13:32–37[2]

[32] But of that day and hour no one knows, not even the angels in Heaven, nor the Son, but only the Father. [33] Take heed, watch and pray; for you do not know when the time is. [34] It is like a man going to a far country, who left his house and gave authority to his servants, and to each his work, and commanded the doorkeeper to watch. [35] Watch therefore, for you do not know when the master of the house is coming—in the evening, at midnight, at the crowing of the rooster, or in

the morning—[36] lest, coming suddenly, he finds you sleeping. [37] And what I say to you, I say to all: Watch!

Verses 35–37 list evening, midnight, early dawn, and late daybreak. Think about your day. What are you usually doing at these points in your day? Would you hear the trumpet call to rise with Him in the air? Or is the busyness of your day drowning out the sound of God?

How much time do we put into planning a wedding, preparing for the birth of a baby, or purchasing or building a new home? Do we place the same importance on preparing for Christ's return? His return is the most important event in our lives, which will last for eternity.

Luke 12:39–40[1] tells us, [39] "Everyone would be ready for him if they knew the exact hour of his return—just as they would be ready for a thief if they knew when he was coming. [40] "So be ready all the time. For I, the Messiah, will come when least expected."

Many have thought the coming of the Lord was going to be in their day of living, and yet we are still talking about it, waiting and watching for Him ourselves. Why is God allowing the return of Christ to be delayed? It's so that more of our loved ones will obtain salvation! Aren't we thankful? Many of us are still praying for our loved ones to receive salvation (2 Peter 3:9).

Since hell is not meant for you and me, God has prepared a way of escape from this eternal torture—salvation, which has already been discussed. Heaven is the home for the righteous. But there is one more topic that needs to be addressed, in case you are still living when it happens. Pray that God finds you faithful and you are not left upon this earth during the tribulation period.

For further study, you may read Matthew 24:36–51; Luke 21:34–36; Matthew 25:13; Matthew 26:38–42; Mark 14:34–38; and 1 Thessalonians 5:1–11.

CHAPTER 32

Rapture and Tribulation Period

WHEN IT COMES TO THE RAPTURE AND TRIBULATION PERIOD, there is ample confusion and division among the churches. It appears that many do not know what to believe. If the believers are not convinced and don't believe anymore, how can we expect unbelievers to understand or convince them of its truth?

Some scholars argue about when Jesus will return and when we will meet Him in the air. If you have heard any teaching or sermons on this subject, then you have heard the term *caught up*—and this term is the reason you will hear believers discussing the Rapture. The word *rapture* in the *Merriam-Webster's Collegiate Dictionary* is defined as "spiritual ecstasy." In the thesaurus section, synonyms for ecstasy are "Heaven, rapture, seventh Heaven, transport."

You may also hear Christians debating the Rapture event happening before the seven-year tribulation period; others believe the Rapture will take place in the middle of the seven-year tribulation period, and yet others believe we will go through the entire seven-year period before we are raptured to Heaven. Why does it matter whether it is pre-trib, mid-trib, or post-trib? If you live every day as if it is your last, you don't worry about what day the Lord is coming back. You just know you are ready—you are prepared.

1 Corinthians 15:50–58[1]: [50] I tell you this, my brothers: an earthly body made of flesh and blood cannot get into God's Kingdom. These perishable bodies of ours are not the right kind to live forever. [51] But I am telling you this strange and wonderful secret: we shall not all die, but we shall all be given new bodies! [52] It will all happen in a moment, in the twinkling of an eye, when the last trumpet is blown. For there will be a trumpet blast from the sky, and all the Christians who have died will suddenly become alive, with new bodies that will never, never die; and then we who are still alive shall suddenly have new bodies too. [53] For our earthly bodies, the ones we have now that can die, must be transformed into Heavenly bodies that cannot perish but will live forever. [54] When this happens, then at last this Scripture will come true—"Death is swallowed up in victory." [55-56] O death, where then your victory? Where then your sting? For sin—the sting that causes death—will all be gone; and the law, which reveals our sins, will no longer be our judge. [57] How we thank God for all of this! It is he who makes us victorious through Jesus Christ our Lord! [58] So, my dear brothers, since future victory is sure, be strong and steady, always abounding in the Lord's work, for you know that nothing you do for the Lord is ever wasted as it would be if there were no resurrection.

1 Thessalonians 4:13–18[1]: [13] And now, dear brothers, I want you to know what happens to a Christian when he dies so that when it happens, you will not be full of sorrow, as those are who have no hope. [14] For since we believe that Jesus died and then came back to life again, we can also believe that when Jesus returns, God will bring back with him all the Christians who have died.

[15] I can tell you this directly from the Lord: that we who are still living when the Lord returns will not rise to meet him ahead of those who are in their graves. [16] For the Lord himself will come down from Heaven with a mighty shout and with the soul-stirring cry of the archangel and the great trumpet-call of God. And the believers who are dead will be the first to rise to meet the Lord. [17] Then we who are still alive and remain on the earth will be caught up with them in the clouds to meet the Lord in the air and remain with him forever. [18] So comfort and encourage each other with this news.

1 Thessalonians 5:1–11[1]: [1]When is all this going to happen? I really don't need to say anything about that, dear brothers, [2] for you know perfectly well that no one knows. That day of the Lord will come unexpectedly, like a thief in the night. [3] When people are saying, "All is well; everything is quiet and peaceful"—then, all of a sudden, disaster will fall upon them as suddenly as a woman's birth pains begin when her child is born. And these people will not be able to get away anywhere—there will be no place to hide. [4] But, dear brothers, you are not in the dark about these things, and you won't be surprised as by a thief when that day of the Lord comes. [5] For you are all children of the light and of the day, and do not belong to darkness and night. [6] So be on your guard, not asleep like the others. Watch for his return and stay sober. [7] Night is the time for sleep and the time when people get drunk. [8] But let us who live in the light keep sober, protected by the armor of faith and love, and wearing as our helmet the happy hope of salvation. [9] For God has not chosen to pour out his anger upon us but to save us through our Lord Jesus Christ; [10] he died for us so that we can live with him forever, whether we are dead or alive at the time of his return. [11] So encourage each other to build each other up, just as you are already doing.

In Matthew 24 and Luke 21, Jesus tells about the future. I love what He said in Matthew 24:36[1]—"But no one knows the date and hour when the end will be—not even the angels. No, nor even God's Son. Only the Father knows"—and verse 42:[1] "So be prepared, for you don't know what day your Lord is coming."

I implore you, be watchful; be ready for when He calls us! Another important part for all of us to remember is this: love each other regardless of what we believe. Unconditional love is what our God gives us and what is required of us to give to others.

Why am I telling you this? It's because I do want you to

miss the seven-year Tribulation period! Remember that God did make a way of escape! In Revelation 3:10, the Word says, "Because you have kept My command to persevere, I also will keep you from the hour of trial which shall come upon the whole world, to test those who dwell on the earth."

Romans 5:8–9:[1] "[8] But God showed his great love for us by sending Christ to die for us while we were still sinners. [9] And since by his blood he did all this for us as sinners, how much more will he do for us now that he has declared us not guilty? Now he will save us from all of God's wrath to come."

See how simple the gospel is? Atheists believe it is only for the simple-minded. Could that be due to its simplicity? Let me take a quote from our daughter as she challenged a college professor regarding the significance of Christianity. She expressed to him, "If *you* are right, I don't have anything to lose. But if *I'm* right, you have everything to lose."

My prayer is for each one of you to have such a divine encounter with Jesus Christ, the Son of the living God, in such a sweet and empowering way that you will run to Him as a child runs into the arms of his loving parents. Only God can change your life for the better. The more intimate you become with our Father, the sweeter His presence becomes. Maybe you have tried the things of this world, yet they have not satisfied your inner longing. Allow Jesus to be the fulfillment of your soul. In John 15:5–8, Jesus said that the only way to live a good life was to stay close to Him. Such a life brings glory to God.

Keep your eyes on the goal of Heaven, for Jesus tells us in

Matthew 25 that there will be a separation and final judgment after the Tribulation period. At this judgment God will either look at you and say, "Come, you blessed of My Father, inherit the kingdom prepared for you from the foundation of the world" (verse 34) or "Depart from Me, you cursed, into the everlasting fire prepared for the devil and his angels" (verse 41).

In John 5:24–30, Jesus begins by saying, "Most assuredly, I say to you," so it makes me take note of His next words. Jesus then tells us that anyone who hears His Word [the Bible] and believes in Him [God] will have eternal life and will not endure judgment.

John 5:28–29:[2] "[28] Do not marvel at this; for the hour is coming in which all who are in the graves will hear His voice [29] and come forth—those who have done good, to the resurrection of life, and those who have done evil, to the resurrection of condemnation."

John 10:10:[2] "The thief [Satan] does not come except to steal, and to kill, and to destroy. I [Jesus] have come that they may have life, and that they may have it more abundantly."

Revelation 22:12:[2] "And behold, I am coming quickly, and My reward is with Me, to give to every one according to his work."

Choose life today! Do not let your family circle be broken with you as the missing piece! Invite Jesus into your heart today!

TREASURES OF THE HEART

What are some of your favorite memories you would pass on to future generations?

TREASURES OF THE HEART

What are some of your favorite memories you would pass on to future generations?

Endnotes

1. All scripture references marked TLB are taken from *Life Application Bible: The Living Bible*; Tyndale House Publishers, Inc. and Youth for Christ USA, Wheaton, Illinois. Copyright 1988.
2. All scripture references marked NKJV (New Kings James Version) are taken from *NKJV Spirit-Filled Life Bible*; Thomas Nelson Books, Nashville, Tennessee. Copyright 1991.
3. *Heaven Is For Real*. Todd Burpo with Lynn Vincent; Thomas Nelson Books.

Printed in the United States
By Bookmasters